ALONE AGAINST THE KLAN

ONE MAN'S FIGHT
FOR JUSTICE

STEVEN H. STOKES, MD

ISBN 979-8-88644-672-2 (Paperback)
ISBN 979-8-88644-673-9 (Digital)

Copyright © 2022 Steven H. Stokes, MD
All rights reserved
First Edition

All rights reserved. No part of this publication may be reproduced, distributed, or transmitted in any form or by any means, including photocopying, recording, or other electronic or mechanical methods without the prior written permission of the publisher. For permission requests, solicit the publisher via the address below.

Covenant Books
11661 Hwy 707
Murrells Inlet, SC 29576
www.covenantbooks.com

DEDICATION

This book is dedicated to T. Larry Smith. Larry has spent the last half of his life researching and preserving the history of Henry County, Alabama. Without Larry's efforts, our heritage would have been lost.

INTRODUCTION

In 2021, my son Jon, who is a personal injury attorney with the firm of Stokes Stemle, asked me to accompany him to visit the new national Memorial for Peace and Justice in downtown Montgomery. The memorial includes a long hall that has approximately five feet long cast iron cylinders resembling bells suspended from the ceiling. Cut into the bells are the names of the victims by state and county. A light inside each bell illuminates the name. This memorial has revitalized the downtown area and is now on the Alabama civil rights trail. It was a moving experience for both Jon and me.

I was drawn to the hall where the names of lynching victims are displayed by state and county. I grew up on a peanut farm in rural Henry County, Alabama, and sought out the Henry County Memorial. There, cut into the metal bell hanging from the ceiling, was the name Wes Johnson, 1937. I had never heard his story.

Each week I visit my elderly aunt, aged eighty-four, who with my deceased mother grew up in Tumbleton. I asked her about the lynching. She replied, "A black man raped a white woman and the Ku Klux Klan took care of him. No one ever wanted to talk about it. Did you know it happened right up the road from our home?"

The following week, I sought out T. Larry Smith, the Henry County local historian. Larry has spent the last half of his life researching, documenting, and preserving local history. I asked Larry about the lynching, and he offered to share the details of the story as he knew them. Larry rode with me to where the tree Wes Johnson had been lynched had stood. He insisted that I not use the name of the Ku Klux Klan members who had shared their stories with him prior to their death, nor the white woman and husband who had alleged rape. Larry felt that this was such a painful incident for this community and the descendants of those involved that I should leave it alone. I have honored Larry's request in not naming some of those involved for the benefit of those descendants who continue to live in Henry County.

This account is tragic, but today with our country's ongoing racial unrest, the story of a prominent white man who tried to protect an innocent black man and stood alone against the fury of the Ku Klux Klan deserves to be told.

Henry County at the Turn of the Century

At the turn of the century, in the early 1900s, Tumbleton was a small crossroads in southern Henry County in southeast Alabama. It was a farming community. A few of the men had joined the army during World War I, serving in the famed rainbow division in France. Following the war, they returned home to mostly farm. A man's status was determined by their ability to own farmland.

Following World War I, farm prices were high. Young men could obtain a loan from a bank or from another successful wealthy individual who could provide the cash to purchase the property. Typically, one man with a mule could work 120 acres and support a family. Following the Civil War, Black families after gaining their freedom typically remained on the land working as sharecroppers for their previous owners. Where else could they go? Without an education, specific skills, or money to relocate, they were stuck on the land. As long as they *knew their place*, everyone got along fine. As an example, when a Black man came to a White person's home, they were expected to use the back door that was off the kitchen and never come to the front door. When riding in a farm truck, Black men or women always sat in the back truck bed, never upfront in the cab with the whites. Blacks were always to address a White man as *sir*.

These daily rituals served to maintain the social structure. For a Black man, the quickest way to get killed was to *mess with a white woman.*

This was a close-knit community. It was not unusual for brothers to marry sisters. When meeting someone new, there were two basic questions: first, what church do you attend? Second, who is your family? In the late summer when farm work slowed, churches would have weeklong *revivals.* Eligible young men and women would attend looking for a possible spouse. An example was my maternal grandmother, a Bradshaw who was one of twelve sisters. Her family lived on a small farm about ten miles from Tumbleton. The oldest sister had married a man who lived near Tumbleton. Each year at revival, as sisters became old enough to marry, they would come for the week to visit. Ultimately, seven of the twelve daughters married men in the Tumbleton area—usually brothers or their cousins. These traditions resulted in families being closely intertwined through marriage and church relationships.

Then the great depression came. Farm prices dropped. Many small farmers who were indebted to a bank or a private lender lost their farms, and the land was repossessed. The Bradshaw family was an example. When the bank came to repossess the farmhouse and its contents along with the land, the elderly mother left her home with nothing but a suitcase containing her clothes. Her husband had been an alcoholic and only survived a short time. For her few remaining years, she moved from daughter to daughter, typically staying two to three weeks. She would then pack her suitcase and move on to another daughter. This was her routine until she died. To lose a farm meant you had two options. First, you could become a tenant farmer or second a sharecropper. A few men were able to find employment working in a dry goods store or perhaps had a skill such as a carpenter, but these options were limited.

A few men with families chose the more difficult option of working in the textile mills in Columbus, Georgia. The new federal road that ran from Columbus, Georgia, to Panama City, Florida, ran through Tumbleton. On Sunday afternoon, a man would take the bus coming through Tumbleton and travel the dirt road north a few hours to Columbus, Georgia. There they worked in the textile mill, sending money home to the family. On Friday night, they would catch the late bus home and spend the weekend with their wife and children who remained in the Tumbleton area. Several families survived for years by this means.

As a tenant farmer, you would live in a small house provided by the landowner. You worked for a set weekly wage. Your wife, in addition to caring for the family, would manage a small family garden, and would help with housework and other domestic duties for the large landowner's wife. The family would survive by having a milk cow, few chickens, and if lucky, maybe a pig. The landowner could fire you and evict your family from the tenet house at any time.

The other option, favored in most cases by the landowner, was that of a sharecropper. The landowner provided you with a small tenet house, or you may have remained in the home that had been yours before you lost your farm. The landowner would provide seed and fertilizer for the coming year's crop. You and your family provided all the labor for the farmland you were assigned by the landowner. The landowner would loan you money to buy food, basic supplies, and clothing, or in most cases you would obtain these necessary items on credit from a store owned and operated by the landowner. As this was the only store within walking distance, you were forced to accept whatever prices were set by the landowner. At the end of the year when the crop was harvested, you would *settle up* and repay your debt to the landowner, and then split any leftover money equally. In most years, there would be little money left over to share.

As a tenant farmer working for wages or as a sharecropper, the life was hard, and you and your family always remained in poverty. Any illness, disability, or injury could be catastrophic, and rarely did you ever get out of debt.

John Harper Oates

John Harper was born in 1882 in the Union Freewill Baptist Church community south of Abbeville. The Oates family was distinguished in the county. William Oates commanded the Civil War volunteers from Abbeville. As part of the 15th Alabama regiment, they fought the second day of Gettysburg at the Battle for Little Round Top. Later in a subsequent battle, Colonel Oates lost his arm from a gunshot wound. Following the war, he served in the US Congress and later as governor of Alabama. John Harper's great grandfather helped establish Abbeville and later founded the town of Geneva. In 1914, at age of thirty-two, John Harper and his first wife Lillie Mae Stokes moved to the small crossroads of Tumbleton. The land there unlike the union community was flat and fertile; it was dotted with many small ponds. As the small ponds were drained, it left rich fertile soil and was some of the best farmland in the state. Members of the union community commented that John Harper's family would be dead within a year from *the fever*, which was common in that area. Tradition was that the roads around Tumbleton were so bad that a loaded wagon could *tumble over*—hence the name Tumbleton. John Harper and Lillie had four children before she died in 1928. He then married Nellie Ruth Thomas, who had been his first wife's private nurse. They had two children together.

John Harper became a successful farmer and businessman. He served as a trustee of the local school. By the 1930s, he had ten or twelve sharecropper families working on his farm. He built them a Black housing area that was called Oates Quarter on the farm. He built a baseball field for the Black children near his home. John Harper donated land for the first and only Black school. He donated land for the Rocky Head Black Baptist Church. He was director of the Farm Bureau, and a stockholder in the Headland peanut oil mill. He was a member of the Browns Crossroads Masonic Lodge #529. He was elected to the Henry County Board of Education, serving as the chairman several terms. He was elected as a Henry County commissioner. In 1936, he was the county campaign manager for the elected democratic governor Bibb Graves. He installed the Oates peanut shelling business and in 1936 was elected to the Henry County Road commission when the county built its first paved road. He was a partner in the Oates and Moring Mercantile business in Abbeville. He built and operated the Oates Mercantile store on his farm that was utilized by the surrounding sharecropper families.

Willie Shelley, my maternal grandfather, was his next-door neighbor and also a member of New Zion Baptist Church. Willie was a small farmer with 120 acres and 1 mule. Every political campaign that John Harper ran, he arranged for Willie to run against him, but Willie never campaigned. He never asked for anyone's vote, never put up a single campaign sign, or went to a campaign rally. Willie always lost, but by being on the ballot, it helped ensure that John Harper avoided any serious opposition and would always be elected.

John Harper was a deacon at New Zion Freewill Baptist Church, the largest church in the Tumbleton community. Small rural Baptist Churches in Henry County could not afford a full-time preacher. The churches would share a minister and held church services on the first and third, or the second and fourth Sundays. If the regularly scheduled preacher was unable to attend church, John Harper would preach the service. Frequently, families requested that John Harper perform the funeral service instead of the preacher for their loved ones. By 1937, he was recognized as a community leader, a *shaker and mover*, and respected by all.

Tumbleton at this time was growing with a population of around 1000. In the late 1920s the new federal highway that ran from Columbus, Georgia, to Panama City, Florida, came through Tumbleton. The increased traffic promoted growth and improved transportation. This is today's 431 and was a main north south route.

One of the many sharecropper families living on the Oates farm was Lee and Bell Johnson. Childless, they had taken in their nephew, an orphan Wes Pearce, and raised him as their own son and he had taken their name. At this time, Wes was eighteen years old, and was described as a large six feet two inches tall strong, athletic young man who was an excellent baseball pitcher. In addition to working on the farm with his uncle and aunt, during the slow winter season when there was not much work to do on the farm, he had a menial job in the nearby town of Headland. Wes would walk from his home on the Oates farm a mile to the main road, where he could catch a ride into Headland each morning for work.

THE KU KLUX KLAN

Society in rural Henry County had been turned upside down by the apocalypse of the Civil War. In 1861, slightly over three hundred men had marched off from Henry County to fight for the confederacy. Four years later at Appomattox, there were twenty-five survivors; the rest were either dead or disabled.

Wives left as widows, or married to a disabled veteran missing an arm or leg or suffering from what today we call PTSD. A society filled with old maids and widows as there were no remaining eligible men to marry. With reconstruction, the former slaves were now in charge. The surviving White men were unable to vote unless willing to sign a loyalty oath, which many of them refused.

The Klan was organized in 1865, initially to regain political power. New Black voters brought the Republican party to prominence controlling all elected offices. The previously disenfranchised Whites as they regained the ability to vote, flocked to the Democratic Party. By the turn of the century, the Democratic Party with almost universal White support had regained political control of most southern states.

The Klan appealed to Whites by promising stability, tradition, Christian values, and held to the myth of the *lost cause*. Southern White families told and retold the story of their sacrifice. They continued to fly the Confederate battle flag, which was incorporated into many state flags as a sign of defiance. My paternal great-great-grandfather lost two brothers in the Civil War. Their commanding officer from Montgomery was a Col. Holt, who was later killed during the war. My grandfather requested that in every generation, a male should have the middle name Holt to remember and honor his commanding officer. Even now, 150 years later, the tradition in my family continues.

In early days, the Klan enforced social stability. If a husband was abusing his wife or not supporting his family, the Klan would pay him a nighttime visit. They would call him out and threaten him with a *horse whipping* if he did not straighten up and take care of the family. The Klan promised a stable, God-fearing vigilante force that would also help regain White domination that had been taken from them. Through the early 1900s, Whites regained political control through literacy requirements, poll taxes to vote, and outright intimidation at polling places to disenfranchise Blacks.

The foot soldiers of the Klan were generally the poorer members of the community. By day, they had little social status or power, but at night dressed in their white robes and hoods as part of a militant band, they were *somebody*. Although a few well-educated, wealthy White men joined the Klan, their affiliation was used by politically astute candidates for public office to help their chances for election. Although relatively small in number, the Klan had a great influence on local elections. It was difficult, if not impossible, to win a county or statewide election without support of the local Klan members.

THE RAPE

Friday, January 29, 1937, was a cold day. This was a slow time of the year for farm labor. Wes Johnson, who lived with his aunt and uncle on John Harper Oates Farm, had a part-time job in Headland. Each morning, he would walk approximately a mile to the main highway between Tumbleton and Headland, and catch a ride to his job. That morning, he was late and missed his ride.

A few miles north just above Tumbleton, Robert and his wife Donna rented a small farmhouse from the owner Bob Smith. Donna, age twenty-three, was originally from Missouri. She had met her husband Robert while he was in the army. They had settled in Tumbleton, renting the farmhouse to be near Robert's family, who lived in nearby Newville. A neighbor's wife stated, "Donna was not one of us."

Robert had suspected that Donna was having an affair with another man. That morning, he left for work as usual, but instead of traveling to Newville a few miles west for work, he hid in some nearby woods near their home. Wes, having missed his ride to work that morning, showed up around noon at the house to see Donna.

Waiting for a short time after Wes had entered his home, Robert quietly slipped back to the house. Barging into the bedroom, he found Wes and Donna in bed. Shouting, "I will kill you both!" Robert rushed the two. In the melee that ensued, Wes was able to free himself and leap out a nearby window. Donna crawled under the bed screaming. After Robert had run out of the house chasing Wes, she ran to the nearby neighbor's wife and confessed of her relationship with Wes, and that Robert had caught them. Robert was a large man over six feet tall weighing nearly three hundred pounds. Donna was wise to fear Robert's wrath. The wife hid Donna in the closet in the event Robert came searching for her.

Robert, after chasing Wes from his home, was not able to keep up, and Wes escaped into the nearby woods. Robert then went to a nearby neighbor shouting that his wife Donna had been raped by a Black man. Quickly, a posse was assembled, and using hunting dogs, Wes was tracked across the fields to John Harper Oates's home. There John Harper, his wife, five children, and Wes barricaded themselves inside the Oates home.

THE SIEGE

Soon, forty or so members of the local Ku Klux Klan had surrounded the Harper home. His house, which still stands today, is a one-story frame home; it has a large wraparound porch. At that time, there was a general store nearby and several small sharecropper homes.

The Klan demanded that John Harper send Wes out for lynching. John Harper refused! Inside, John Harper armed with a double-barreled shotgun, protected his wife, five children, and Wes. Outside, the Klan numbering forty to fifty men surrounded the house. They were shooting their guns in the air, many drinking moonshine out of mason jars, yelling for John Harper to send Wes out. For the next day and a half, the standoff continued. Day and night, this routine continued without relief. None of John Harper's church members or even his good friend Willie came to his aid; he stood alone. No one could enter or leave the house, but John Harper and his family could not hold out forever. Their water came from an open well out in the yard. It was winter, and the house was heated by an open fireplace. Wood for the fireplace was stored out in the yard. The toilet for the house was an outhouse out in the yard. The Klan, wanting blood, was out in the yard waiting.

It is one thing to lynch an unarmed black man, but something else to break into the home of one of the most respected men in the county. They could easily have broken in the door and rushed inside, possibly killing John Harper, but the first man through the door would have had his guts splattered on the wall by John Harper's double barrel 12-gauge shotgun. The Klan was pouring some whiskey courage out of their mason jars, but there was not enough courage in a mason jar filled with whiskey to break through his door and face a shotgun.

Sunday morning, January 31, Louie Corbett, the Henry County sheriff, drove up to John Harper's house. It is unknown who drove to Abbeville and notified the sheriff of the siege at John Harper's house. Perhaps a neighbor, or more likely the Klan themselves as a means to end the siege. He informed John Harper that he had come to arrest Wes Johnson on the charge of raping Donna. John Harper could not refuse the lawful order of the elected sheriff. He brought Wes out, turning him over to Sheriff Corbett. He was assured by the sheriff that he would protect Wes and that Wes would get a trial. This calmed the situation down, and Sheriff Corbett returned with Wes to Abbeville, locking him in the Henry County jail.

Monday the following day, the Klan summoned their soldiers from throughout the county. That night about fifty armed men assembled in Tumbleton and drove to Abbeville over the dirt road, arriving just after midnight. Abbeville was the county seat with the courthouse in the center of town, surrounded by a town square. The square was surrounded by several small stores, a drugstore, and a café. Customers were in the café that night when the Klan arrived. The Klan, in full uniform of white hoods and robes, paraded around the square with torches, firing their guns into the air, and yelling while the terrified citizens hid. After a few circuits around the square, they proceeded to the county jail a block away where Wes was being held.

There, the current Sheriff Louie Corbett was *asleep* upstairs. Previously, Louis's father JN had been the sheriff, and Louis had been his father's jailer. At the last election, they had traded places, and the former three-term sheriff J. N. Corbett was now the jailer to his son Louie. The armed Klan came inside, and according to both Louie and JN, the Klan held them at gunpoint. Neither the sheriff nor jailer resisted. Not asking for the keys to the cell, the Klan simply forced the door open with a crowbar and took Wes outside to a waiting car. With his arms tied behind him, he was placed in the back of a sedan and driven the thirty minutes back to Tumbleton.

THE EXECUTION

A member of the Klan present that evening related his story to a local historian before he died of natural causes. Wes was put in the back of a sedan with his hands tied behind him. As he was driven down the highway from the jail to Tumbleton, he was punched repeatedly in the face and beaten about the head. The Klan caravan drove to the house where the attack was alleged to have occurred. Across the dirt road at the front of the house was a deep ditch, and on the far bank stood a solitary oak tree. Wes was dragged out of the car and stood up on the side of the road on the edge of the ditch. He never cried, begged for mercy, or said a word. He just stood there bleeding, waiting for the end.

The leader of the Klan called Robert forward and said, "Since you were wronged, you get the first shot." Robert, stepping forward, shot Wes at point blank range. Wes fell backward into the deep ditch. The remainder of the mob gathered at the edge of the ditch and unloaded their shotguns, pistols, and rifles into his still body. Two men then climbed down into the ditch, put a noose around his neck, and hoisted him up for all to see. It was decided that Wes would hang there as a warning to any other black man and a message to others demonstrating what happens when you *messed with a white woman.*

Later that Tuesday morning, word began to spread throughout the community that a young black man was hanging by the neck from a tree limb on the side of the road across from the house where the rape had occurred. A laughing half-drunk group of Klan men stood guard at the tree to prevent anyone taking the body down for burial. A reporter for the local newspaper *The Dothan Eagle* was called and came to the scene for the story. On February 4, the image of Wes hanging from the tree appeared in the local paper along with the story.

Wes's mother, Bell, was washing clothes for Mrs. Blanche Knight that morning. Blanche's husband George ran a small store in Tumbleton. When George heard of the murder, he closed his store and drove home to tell his wife, Blanche. She then went out to the yard and told Bell that she needed to go over to Mr. John Harper's house, not mentioning the murder. Bell knew something was wrong and cried out, "Lord mercy, they have killed him." She took off running across the fields to John Harper's house half a mile away.

Around noon, John Harper, with two of his black sharecropper field hands, took his flatbed farm truck and drove to the tree where Wes was hanging. There, several of the Klan stood guard to prevent Wes's body from being taken down for burial. When John Harper pulled up with his truck for the body, they stood aside.

John Harper and his two men placed Wes's body on the truck bed, covered him with a sheet, and drove to Little Rocky Mount Colored Free Will Baptist Church. John Harper had donated land to the church several years ago for the building and the cemetery. There, Wes was buried in an unmarked grave known only to the church members. There was fear that the Klan would return and desecrate the cemetery or vandalize the church.

For weeks after the lynching, there was fear the Klan would target others in the community. When Black families came to Tumbleton to buy their weekly food and other essential supplies, they came as a group. The women and children huddled in the center with the men around the periphery as protection. As a group, they waited outside the stores in the street, until they had their food and then walked home again huddled in a group. But slowly, life resumed its normal rhythm.

JUSTICE

Alabama Democratic Governor Bibb Graves, himself a Klan member, was quick to react. The governor stated, "Alabama would not tolerate mob violence." He ordered a full inquiry into the lynching and called for the guilty men to be brought to justice.

On Thursday, February 4, Governor Graves ordered Judge Hallstead of Headland to call a special session of the Henry County grand jury to be held the following Friday and Saturday in Abbeville. The Governor also ordered papers of impeachment to be filed against Sheriff Louie Corbett. On Friday, February 5, a string of witnesses paraded into the jury room in the Abbeville courthouse. Judge Hallstead stressed that mob violence was a threat to society. Several Tumbleton residents were called to testify, but no one knew anything. Amazingly, no one could identify any of the Klan members.

After two days of testimony concerning the lynching of Wes Johnson, the special grand jury failed to indict anyone. On Saturday, February 6, the final verdict read, "We have failed to return an indictment against anyone in connection with this matter. Inasmuch as impeachment proceedings have already been ordered against the sheriff of our County, we deem it inadvisable to investigate his conduct. What he did or did not do to protect the prisoner, Wes Johnson, and prevent his being taken from the county jail and killed, we therefore have nothing to report on this matter, one way or another. In our judgment, the other officers of this court have not been negligent in any manner in the performance of their duty, we now await the orders of the court."

Later in the year, Governor Graves ordered a new grand jury in Montgomery to indict the members of the Klan and impeach Sheriff Corbitt. That grand jury also declined to indict anyone—so one day there would be justice for all, but not on this day.

HENRY COUNTY

John Harper and his wife, Ruth, raised their five children, some of whom still live in Henry County. In life, we are sometimes faced with doing what is right or doing what is easy. Doing what is right comes with a price. John Harper, prior to this event, was considered an up and coming political *shaker and mover*. After his defense of Wes Johnson against the Klan, he was a marked man. For his defiance of the Klan, he was not elected to a county-wide office again until 1951 when elected as county commission chairman. In 1954, John Harper appeared on WSFA, a television station in Montgomery, where he was recognized as one of Alabama's outstanding citizens. He died of cancer at the age of eighty-four and is buried in the cemetery of his beloved New Zion Baptist Church in Tumbleton. His was a life well-lived.

Robert and Donna remained married. They raised two children, lived out their lives without further incident, and are buried in the community.

In 2022, Governor Bibb Graves's name was removed from the campus building honoring him by the University of Alabama trustees. This for his involvement with the Ku Klux Klan.

Sheriff Louie Corbett, despite allowing Wes Johnson, a prisoner in his care, to be taken by the Klan and murdered, did not harm his political career. He was elected for three additional terms serving as sheriff through 1955.

Wes Johnson remained in an unmarked grave in the cemetery at Rocky Head Free Will Baptist Church. Prior to her demise, an elderly aunt identified his grave. Recently, Steve Hardwick, a member of the Henry County historical society, at his expense, placed a stone grave marker at Wes's grave.

Following World War II, there were opportunities up north for both poor White and Black sharecroppers. The county was depopulated with outward migration to northern industries. The population contracted from 22,800 in 1932 to a low 14,000 in 1970. Today, there has been slow recovery of population back to 17,000. Farming is now mechanized and no longer depends on low-paid subsistence sharecroppers. This is a good thing!

Although there was no justice for Wes, may he finally rest in peace. Many of our nation's great civil rights battles were fought in Alabama. The voting rights march from Selma to Montgomery, and Dr. King's Montgomery bus boycott after Rosa Parks' refusal to give up her seat on a city bus to a White man. Today our state's number 1 tourist destination is the Dr. George Washington Carver Museum on the campus of Tuskegee Institute. Today, there are many elected African-American officials in Henry County at all levels of government, and there is racial peace. Finally, there is economic opportunity and justice for all.

School for children of Black Sharecroppers on
land donated by John Harper Oates.

Rocky Head Baptist Church on land donated by John Harper Oates.
Wes Johnson's grave is in cemetery.

National Memorial for Peace and Justice Gallery
of Lynching Victims—Montgomery, AL
https://museumandmemorial.eji.org/memorial

National Memorial for Peace and Justice Gallery
of Lynching Victims—Montgomery, AL
https://museumandmemorial.eji.org/memorial

Abbeville Courthouse—Early 1920's Site of Torch Light Caravan
Wes Johnson taken from Henry County Jail at night and murdered.

John Harper Oates—Age 72 years old

Wes Johnson as pictured in Dothan Eagle—Feb. 1937

Wes Johnson grave site.
Rocky Head Baptist Church—2022

John Harper Oates home—2022
Site of siege by Ku Klux Klan.

New Zion Free Will Baptist Church—where John Harper
Oates served as Deacon and stand-in Preacher.
He is buried in this cemetery.

Tumbleton, Alabama

Unincorporated community

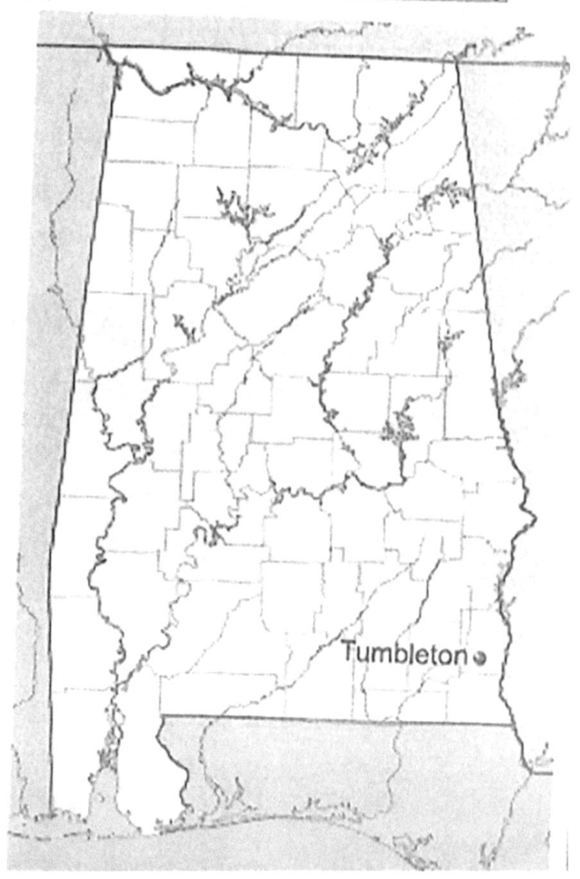

Location of Tumbleton in Henry County, AL

ABOUT THE AUTHOR

Steve grew up on a small pea-nut farm in rural Southeast Alabama. He attended Auburn University on an ROTC scholarship. Upon graduation, he chose the United States Marine Corps. After completing infantry school, he attended army ranger school where he was an honor graduate. He then commanded a recon platoon and company with Vietnam service.

After completing his military obligation, he attended the University of South Alabama College of Medicine and had subsequent residency training in radiation oncology at Washington University in St. Louis. He returned home to Dothan, Alabama, where he was in practice for over thirty years. He served on the Dothan City commission for two terms. He was elected as chairman of Dothan City school board serving one term. Currently, he practices part-time at Florida Cancer Affiliates in Panama City, Florida. Steve continues to volunteer at a free medical clinic for the homeless, work-release prisoners, and with women housed at the House of Ruth for abused women and children.

Active in his church, he has participated for over twenty years with medical missions in Central and South America. He has received the Humanitarian of the Year award by the Rotary Club and most recently, the Medical Society of Alabama. He serves on the Board of Trustees at University of South Alabama, including as past chairman of the board. Currently, he serves as chairman of the Alabama Medical Marijuana Commission.

He is married to his wife, Angelia, of forty-eight years. They have three sons and three grandchildren.

www.ingramcontent.com/pod-product-compliance
Lightning Source LLC
Chambersburg PA
CBHW020852160726

47993CB00004B/1622